HORAN'S FIELD AND OTHER RESERVATIONS

The AE Memorial Award of £100, made every fifth year for 'the best literary work, either creative or scholarly, by an Irish writer under thirty-five' was awarded to the author in December 1945. Many of the poems in the manuscript which received the award were subsequently published as the volume 'Reservations' by *Envoy*. Seven hundred and fifty copies were printed, of which four hundred were for sale in Ireland. Over three hundred copies appeared under the imprint of the MacMillan Co., Ltd. (London). A number of copies appeared in the U.S.A. under the imprint of the Saint Martin's Press.

VALENTIN IREMONGER

HORAN'S FIELD
AND OTHER RESERVATIONS

THE DOLMEN PRESS

*Set in Times Roman type, and
printed and published in the Republic of Ireland at the
Dolmen Press Limited, 8 Herbert Place, Dublin 2.*

1972

*Distributed outside Ireland, except in Canada and in the United States of America
by Oxford University Press.*

SBN 85105 212 6

Contents

All in the end
for Sheila naturally

Acknowledgements

Acknowledgements are due to the editors of the following magazines in whose pages these poems first appeared: *The Bell, The Irish Times, Irish Writing, Envoy, The Listener, The Kenyon Review, (U.S.A.);* and also to the B.B.C. and Radio Eireann.

Backward Look

Looking at stones and airguns I recall my childhood
Spent among tin-cans, gravel-heaps and dead walls,
And the strand at Sandymount, where the tide reminded
Me of the outside newspaper world.

But my world was private and immense enough then:
Its statemen had torn jerseys and great vocabularies,
Though the words that hurtled from their mouths were the parents' fears
Pathologically transmitted to their sons

Who herded together in armies and elected leaders
And were instinctively kind in their frequent wars:
Being anxious about the wounded, abandoning hostilities
When pellets or stones or sods of grass drew tears.

The depredation of orchards was the intuitive beginning
Of the later scramble for food: though the well-earned fruits were communal,
Sharing of profits being the natural order of things
In that world where our hopes were neighbours and friendly.

These now are gibbering days. My head is in iron.
I walk around in a rank and dare not break it.
My minutes move on to a fate they cannot retard.
I look at the gun they have given me and am sad.

1941.

The Toy Horse

Somebody, when I was young, stole my toy horse,
The charm of my morning romps, my man's delight.
For two days I grieved, holding my sorrow like flowers
Between the bars of my sullen angry mind.

Next day I went out with evil in my heart,
Evil between my eyes and at the tips of my hands,
Looking for my enemy at the armed stations,
Until I found him, playing in his garden

With my toy horse, urgent in the battle
Against the enemies of his Unreason's land:
He was so happy, I gave him also
My vivid coloured crayons and my big glass marble.

Girl in a Red Dress

The bitch-eyed girl spoke to me warily
And more than a hand stirred my silk hair.
She had a red dress that was high-fashioned
By craftsmen glad of her casual favour

And low-tongued in exile were the virtuous ladies
Who had dangled their laughs at me with serious intention.
I spoke little to her, just answered her greeting,
Yet by night I knew that she was not a maid.

Now, though Heaven is witness that I did not wish it happen,
May the Lord retain me in the mood of this girl-eyed bitch
Who tears up my days and offers me no right compensation
For the stripped and spiked bone's-end of my mind she blunted.

White, White Flower

My flower was white and had beautiful petals,
A long, tough stalk, a green centre.
My mother gave it to me after breakfast,
Picking it specially in our own garden.

I walked in the streets with it, a shy hero,
Holding it in my left hand, a symbol of victory,
Knowing I had earned it but afraid of people
Looking, who would laugh at me for my simplicity.

They did not jeer but in their midst accepted me,
Me with my white flower and strange long fingers,
Me with my clumsy body and my peculiar slouch
And the awkwardness of nature in my eyes.

So I went to one that I thought loved me, thinking
She will like this flower my mother has given me,
And, taking it as a love-token, keep it
Later between a book's pages.

She was sitting in the window looking downstreet.
When she saw me, she burst out laughing.
Running towards me she took the flower and, laughing,
Tore it, breaking the beautiful petals.

Dark Way

It is dark here and there are ghosts roving
Up and down among the trees and by the roadway.
Come closer, my darling, and let me guard you
From the evil that is round us and threatening.

These are the shapes of our wicked fancies
That, baulked in the daytime, gather round at night
With their terrible accusations and their gross demands,
Their exhortations and their meaning looks.

We recognise the things we never did,
Sins of omission, thoughtlessness that caused
Pain to others, the dross of our being
That, gathering behind the skin, now bursts outwards.

Come the morning redness of the day we'll find
These things have returned to their natural graves
Behind the blaséness of eyes and fingers,
The controlled nostrils and the firm mouth.

But we now, the big-eyed travellers, must forge ahead,
Prepared to meet these things each following night.
How can we figure out the blasé answers, having
No artificial daylight for the mind?

Soldier from the Wars

Somebody, I gather, is fishing in Galway,
In afternoon drift on the Corrib's lower reaches,
Hooking deftly the wet fish, returning
Easily to tea at sundown.

He is, I think, a young man with girls in his eyes —
Afternoon tennis and romantic late-night dances,
Hoping to meet later the gallant girl, marry,
Have two children, live comfortably in the country.

He has survived Dunkirk and the Grecian islands,
Coming unscathed to fight on the cliffs of Crete
And after in Africa, to and fro across the desert,
Seeking the promised land of his happiness.

And he has known also his private danger,
The ugly nip in the night from the crab-like claws
Of *Why didn't I do it* and *What should I say,*
Through the strait hours and no answer.

And now, eluding London and the swinging girls,
He comes to this backwater to attempt to hook
The five-foot-ten of happiness which is his birthright
Before his blood trumpets a more insidious war.

Whom I heard of casually in a Dublin bus, to this
Unknown young man my hand reaches, to answer
The wishes in his sinews and behind his eyes,
Unspoken in the gardens of his longing.

I pray that this unknown young man who has known
The lightning's strict hour, the time of anger
And the thunder within, may know also
The peace following always the days of action.

14

May he survive unscathed the Dunkirk of middle-age
And cardiac decay, the Crete of married life,
The Peloponnese-like archipelagoes of children, to fish lazily
In the reaches of a quiet old age.

A Pane of Glass

The roadmenders outside my window sit all day
Hammering the paving stones to a definite shape
So that no fine lady or gallant gentleman should ignominiously
Be tripped or upset on the wet and muddy streets.

And I all day behind my window with a pen
In my right hand sit and add up figures,
Or write long threatening letters to schoolteachers guilty
Of indiscretions really of no consequence.

A pane of glass divides the air between us, makes
Two worlds of one: a close examination will reveal
Flaws in the glass that, lingering on the cornea,
Distort for each the other's world and his own.

What but to break the glass and unhampered let me chip
My life to the required smooth even shape
And let the roadmender, if he so wishes, balance
The account of his days and threaten all the bosses.

Gulls

The gulls bank back, daunted. Like a steamer
The wind destroys the sea's still even calm.
Under its monstrous caresses waves chop and menace
And we are aware of storm.
O gulls, gulls, brave ones, back like a parabola curve
In landwards home to your sheltered rock niches.
The morning glowers like an angry child but who can say
If anger will vanish at the sun's first sneaking kindness?
Later there will be time to think of the stress and strain
Of storm but now the safety of the cliff's face beckons.

So, too, my desires, arrowing birds
Native to my life's oceanic quietness,
Not daunted but with the instinct of self-protection
Before society's wrecking ill-natured storm-winds
Which tear and rip my natural morning's joy,
Swerve back to the mind's steep riddled cliff
To fret and fume in its gullies and black chasms.

This Houre Her Vigill

Elizabeth, frigidly stretched,
On a spring day surprised us
With her starched dignity and the quietness
Of her hands clasping a black cross.

With book and candle and holy water dish
She received us in the room with the blind down.
Her eyes were peculiarly closed and we knelt shyly
Noticing the blot of her hair on the white pillow.

We met that evening by the crumbling wall
In the field behind the house where I lived
And talked it over, but could find no reason
Why she had left us whom she had liked so much.

Death, yes, we understood: something to do
With age and decay, decrepit bodies;
But here was this vigorous one, aloof and prim,
Who would not answer our furtive whispers.

Next morning, hearing the priest call her name,
I fled outside, being full of certainty,
And cried my seven years against the church's stone wall.
For eighteen years I did not speak her name

Until this autumn day when, in a gale,
A sapling fell outside my window, its branches
Rebelliously blotting the lawn's green. Suddenly, I thought
Of Elizabeth, frigidly stretched.

1943.

Alone by Night

In the room, between the lamplight and the door's shadow,
My fear stands, monstrous as a naked man,
Clutching the night of the air like a brief cudgel
Over the turmoil of my bleeding past.

I have forgotten how the bright girls danced
Here with a rustle of skirts and a soft laugh.
It is so long since they left this castle,
Not liking the dross and the dirt of its unswept halls.

My eyes follow only the lurching movements
Of this ill-shaped fury, this mountainous bawd,
Who has jumped the claim of my joy and laughter
And frightened away the happy girls.

Between the two eyes I shot him several times
And went back to my books and picked up my pen;
But before nightfall he was capering before me
More insistent and ugly with the angry wounds.

What shall I do, O heart, O heart?
How shall I escape through a locked door?
He has smashed the furniture, my only defences,
And there is no refuge on the floor.

Cross Guns Bridge

Once too often for my taste I shall cross
That bridge two miles north of Dublin where
On one side an orphanage, other, a gas-station,
Stand like twin guardian demons on this undoubting road.

Had they been chosen, what could be more appropriate
On the approach to a graveyard than these two buildings?
Some surrealist impulse welled up like spring-water
And tossed out this gas-station, this bridge and this orphanage.

There, opposite but more than similar, they stand, fit symbols:
One to remind the mourners how they all are homeless
Like the homeless one in the brass-bound coffin whom they follow
From the hub of life to the rim of clay-stopped quietness

And one to tell them how the days rush by,
The acceleration of seconds, the whining meanness of years,
How our minds run dry, how our lives start pinking,
How we need the hands of love to set them right again.

Not London Bridge of London Town but a decrepit structure
Spans the artificial river dividing city and cemetery,
Dividing dead and not-so-dead. It will collapse
Any day and a good many be caught unwittingly.

Yet who would anticipate evil in days like these
When it alights around us like birds unexpectedly
And steals through our chimneys and windows with the day
Of the light and the night of the dark as its cloaks.

Well to the south of Dublin, to-day I watch
The evening cloud over, the inclination of rain.
Outside my window, the green spume of the earth
Drenches the irises of my eyes and my girl is laughing.

On Sandymount Strand

These long years
Watching the seagulls bank and retreat daily
And the tide's remorseless flowing on the wrinkled
Forehead of the strand, I have been happy here,
Stealing apples from orchards and being chased,
Playing football and more mysterious games
Lost to me now, or breaking my heart
For a girl who broke her eight-year life she was so eager
To live and to experience everything well.

And there was poetry. When I found
Lines detonating in my mind and my pen
Stabbing the pages of my memory, I would have sold
My sister to the devil for a poem
Complete and lucid as spring-water, to startle
God and rock his golden throne.
It never came; yet I was happy, too,
With the snapping swords of words and the shields of tinsel phrases.

Gone, now, the adolescent swagger and closed
The book of my youth, ruled, and a trial
Balance extracted for my future use.
I thought to-day
As still the gulls banked and the evil tide
Crept nearer from the horizon while I walked
By Sandymount Tower, now decrepit and strewn
With rubble borne there by the wind and water,
How my youth wore down like an old shoe-sole
Sodden with age,
Leaving between me and the hostile, hard
Ground of society, nothing — nothing at all
Now to prevent the damp and the needling chill
Eating into my bones and burrowing to my heart.

July Evening — Storm Coming Up

On the water the accumulation of spume,
The hiss and purl of spiralling waves, the skid
And visible snarl of wind, horizon's disintegration,
The glower and sharp glint of a tired sky.

Nearer home, between my hand and the breaking water,
The inclination of leaves, the gnarled and aloof
Trunk of an old tree and, under my window,
The yellow disaster of forsythia. The first raindrops fall,
Papers disarray, curtains behave like flags.

Now for the decisions of night, the heart's undoing:
The time where reason and emotions meet.

New Year Bells

Whether to bow a failure out
Or usher another failure in
The bells their murmurings begin
Is more than my pen can denote.

Perhaps this vile Dean, reeling round
The vestry in his night-shift,
Urging the mad bell-ringers sound,
Answers that each new year's gift
Is pain and strife and bursting heads?

But that was in another century;
And, of course, the man is dead.

Shadows

Among the tall heroes are none to understand
How the lightning terrifies and the thunder hurts,
How behind the appalling couch and the rigid high chairs
Devils crouch, snarling, waiting for their meal.

Locked in the cupboard on the top landing
For sure there are dragons, rampant and terrible,
And what horrible gnomes, over and under the bed,
Menace the unconscious hours with their bald shrieking.

Little boy, little boy, learn to be alone,
To grasp courage like straws and float on your fear
With the relaxed wariness of the swimmer, trained
To watch the threatening wave and the deceptive current,

For, in the banquet-hall, at the gay reception,
Walking at night with your girl-friend or alone in your room,
You will have terror, like days, with you all the years of your life
And, among the tall strangers, none will understand.

Underworld

Under this stone, flat, grey, undistinguished
From any other stone in this desolate village
Among the green decay, remnant of a proud
Fall of rain, descant of spring, clear aria
Of water faltering on frond of valley, falling,

There is an urgency of movement, unexpected
Like the blunt stab of sunlight into a dark room,
And where in the sunray from darkness is seen
The world of dust, its frightening industry,
The silence and the swiftness of its menace,

So, under this familiar stone, the unguessed movements,
The reeling zigzags, the back-and-forward dartings
Importune our understanding, our stunned concern.
Something terrible is here we had not dreamt of,
We had not allowed for in our calculations:

The hungry importance of life is precise here beneath
The veneer of decay, the riotousness of moss — a tailpiece
Of truth, a scut of beauty.
                          Lay back the stone.
It is late for walking these savage lanes.
Something unknown is doing something unknowable,
Building, perhaps, a better poor world for its progeny.

Dirge for the Living Self

Iron and sticks to cover my bones,
Money for drinks and a murmuring priest —
Why won't they let me rest in peace?

Where is the girl-eyed boy I loved
Whose hair I tossed with shy intention
And never made him my confession?

Six years down with fingers cramped
He busies himself with tubers and weeds
And roots spat out by unknown seeds.

O dead man, to kiss you now
I rip the skies and strip the earth
And join in everybody's mirth

But when the glass is at my lips
And when my true love gaily cries
Your knuckles iron out my eyes.

Night, again Night

So still have I no rest from these barbed prongs
That mutter in the mind's high flesh and form:
The heart's sharp weapons that attack, deface
The curved sheer beauty of my reason's mould.

On my lips by day the laugh, the glittering
Words deploy, advance along the heart's terrain,
And all the snipers of sentimentality retreat
Before the mind's tough well-trained soldiery.

Yet at night by the dead light
Of the mind's unreason, traitorous friend,
The heart's battalions raise triumphant flags
And pitch their tents among my brain's tilled fields.

So do the castles of my delight kneel down,
The melancholy scavengers of fear come in
To brush the jagged grit of my happiness around
The eye-holes of my madness, my jerking head.

Song

I bring you laughs and keep the tears myself
As I walk to you across the night
Who are the rich orchard of my delight,
My fount of happiness, my wishing well

And all the pears of your aloofness fall
To gabble in these hot gardens like bursting children
Who glimpsed the daring of the witches' cauldron
And to their own burning gave no thought at all.

Love, I have wandered like a blinded Jew,
And now, over the night, my promised land,
You wait for me, kiss in hand,
As lithely I step the remaining miles to you

Who can pin the winds like any insolent Spaniard
Or pierce the tide's malignant eye
With the needle of your happiness and joy.
So, while to-night you are the fine vanguard

To cut the yellow harvest of my years
That flowers in the valley
Of my stony agony,
I bring you laughs; I store away the tears.

Stony Soil

Locked under the clay the seed uncoils
Slowly, in late spring, under a fair sun,
The first efforts at roots, the shy tendrils touching
The unembarrassed earth, softly, oh! gently,
With April tentative music of finch and blackbird.

And later under the sun's outspoken encouragement,
With youth's fine confidence these growing roots
Grip and twine round and hug the yielding soil,
Bolder the advances, rougher the caresses.
The denial of winter will soon be made good:

Autumn shall see the final vehemence
Of seed and soil shocked in their last embrace,
The male arrogance of corn, the pulsing,
Singing sap in root and drunken flower,
The sensuous triumph, the acclamation of leaves.

But here is stony soil: my life's short roots
Snap and break off in society's tough earth.
So spring and winter are the same to me
Whose seed is stunted with the year's advance.
I have no hands to mutter how I cry
Or love to guard the tendrils of my days.

The Choice

It is too much for a man to be alone
All the time, equating laugh with moan,
Anger with joy, white sand with rigid stone,

Attempting to resolve a half-known equation,
Appraising the why and wherefore of his situation,
But always with the personal reservation.

That way madness lies. A tired Dean here
In Dublin, two centuries ago, year by year,
Heard approach the thunder and voiced his fear

Yet could not, though she waited to receive
Him eagerly with tenderness, make himself believe
Happiness as other than being well-deceived.

Good-Time Girl

'No,' she said, 'Why should I? I don't want
To settle down. I'm only twenty-three.
I've got a dream of ribbons in my hair
And dances at the cross-roads, gay and free.

Him? Oh, he understands. He knows a girl
Must stagger out a verse to make a rhyme.'
I thought of Empson and Anita Loos:
A girl can't keep on laughing all the time.

Someone should tell her how the years drip down
Like water from a leaking cistern, wearing out
The patience of the best; and how the silver
Mirror gives no occasion for regret.

Well, I Declare

So many of them, in their impressive attitudes,
Standing under the architraves of the day and the night,
Have spoken pointedly to us and with concern,

Splitting the hairs of logic, that all turned sour
On the tongues of our minds and our eyes wandered
Like schoolchildren's under the earnest teacher,

And it appears now to us that there is no justification
Either for optimism or pessimism as they discuss
The metaphysical necessity for the historical approach,

Who have cheated us of our houses and the broad acres
Our fathers designed for us, leaving us only
The leaking barns and doss-houses of our future.

Let us resolve, then, each, not to be put upon,
To have no truck with anger or apathy, to accept
No man's word for anything: not even for God:
Not even our own.

The Dog

All day the unnatural barking of dogs
Sounded in my ears. In O'Connell Street, among the crowds,
A dog barked at my heels but, when I looked, was gone.
Sitting at my window, later, at nearly three o'clock,
Glad for the quiet harmony of the afternoon,
A voice reached up like a long arm out of the street
To rap on the shutters of my ears but, when I looked,
The street's chaste line was unbroken, its perspective unstrained.

Now, lying awake in bed, smoking,
Looking out the window, I can see him,
Lean-faced and shaggy, as the moonlight falls
Sideways into my room as into a chapel,
Where he squats on the lawn and tilts his lonely snout,
Raising his lost unnatural cry.

God send his master is not dead or none he loves,
Being out of countenance, has sent him for succour
And that I don't understand his plaintiveness:
But yet, God help me, I fear this unnatural barking
Has something to do with me and not with strangers,
As quietly I lie, hearing the hours tick by,
And the unsatisfied dog, howling upon the lawn,
Breaking the night's maidenhead.

Spring Jag

for Avril Webb, 1944.

Spring stops me suddenly like ground
Glass under a door, squeaking and gibbering.
I put my hand to my cheek and the tips
Of my fingers feel blood pulsing and quivering.

A bud on a branch brushes the back
Of my hand and I look, without moving, down.
Summer is there, screwed and fused, compressed,
Neat as a bomb, its casing a dull brown.

From the window of a farther tree I hear
A chirp and a twitter: I blink.
A tow-headed vamp of a finch on a branch
Cocks a roving eye, tips me the wink

And, instantly, the whole great hot-lipped ensemble
Of buds and birds, of clay and glass doors,
Reels in with its ragtime chorus, staggering
The theme of the time, a jam-session's rattle and roar,

With drums of summer jittering in the background
Dully and, deeper down and more human, the sobbing
Oboes of autumn falling across the track of the tune,
Winter's furtive bassoon like a sea-lion snorting and bobbing.

There is something here I do not get,
Some menace that I do not comprehend
Yet so intoxicating is the song
I cannot follow its thought right to the end.

So up the garden path I go with spring
Promising sacks and robes to rig my years
And a young girl to gladden my heart in a tartan
Scarf and freedom from my facile fears.

Spring Stomp

Now while the early sun
Smears the fields with morning,
I will ask my love to come
Trucking down the dawn,
As spring's advance live agents
Of buds and migrant birds
Herald a summer coming
Like thunder from the south.

O love, when we suffer under
Our autumn's cruel regime,
What laws can quell the rebel
Armies of memory,
Or stop the broken lines
Of poems streeling through
The wasted fields of our
Imagination's farms?

So, love, let you come dancing
Down the jazzy lanes of spring,
Through the ragtime green of meadows
By the high cliff's muted brink.
Let's swing it by the river
To the torch-song of the water
While yet our sinews answer
The off-beat's hot-licked pause.

Reservations

'Twenty crocuses in my garden to-day', she said,
'I know spring is here.' She lay on the bed,
Happily, while I stood at the window, sideways,
Thinking, 'This is how it has been always:

Somebody else has been happy because spring was here,
Lazily turning on a bed, smiling. The mere
Veneer of acquiescence was all I ever possessed.'
I know there is a lot that I have missed,

Yet, afraid of March gales, there was nothing I could do
But agree, with reservations — remembering, too,
How winter struck us dumb, not so long ago,
And how it would pay us back for spring, blow for blow.

Descending

'I'm going down,' she said, tying her yellow scarf,
While I still watched the dull grey mountain road
Mooch down into the glen and disappear
Round a curve of trees and cottages. Some sudden fear
Made me not reply or make any attempt to start
Yet awhile; I sat on the old sacrificial stone

To which we had climbed all the hot morning together,
Choosing the difficult way, along the dried-up river bed
Choked with dead boulders covered with a fur of spruce leaves.
Not even the sacrifice of our youth — made at noon — redeems
The swinging boughs of our minds, gay with feathers,
Lopped from us now. 'I'm going down,' she said.

Her teeth were hedges of dense, white sloe-blossom,
Her hair a development of black. Down the afternoon
From the rare peak of youth, too, we are going, to the valley
Of age, lurching and stumbling down its gothic alleys
And grotesque approaches. 'I'm going down.' The gossip
Of the wind in her hair will be stopped much too soon.

A Marriage Has Been Arranged

'Yes,' she said, 'I am happy,' turning the ring
On her finger three times for luck. Spring
Outside the window, ticked off winter who was beyond retorting.
The curtains blew inwards and upwards softly
As she stood, gazing at something I could not see
Far beyond the small pond and the crooked walnut tree.

I was glad for her but could not restrain
A thread of sorrow being pulled through my brain.
How she would marry and decay into contentment
Occasioned in me some amount of resentment
Against the ways and means of our emotional lives,
Their sharp and cunningly concealed knives.

The problem, of course, is to hold this minute Now
In perpetuo while growing ourselves to ripeness; how
To have Time held up by some blunt traffic cop
So letting us, the unfortunate pedestrians, across.
It can't be done, I suppose; so I wish her, my dear,
As much happiness as she can conveniently bear.

The Coming Day

'Every man has his price.' The cyclist rode by
His comment to his comrade on the rackets
Of politics and business nuzzling in my ears.
I walked steadily on, hands in dustcoat pockets,
Knowing that, no matter how much I tried,
I could not stop the thought that slipped and veered

By the foreshore of my mind like a water-wag
Disturbing the calm of my sleep for nights to come
Or tilting the horizon-line of my day and age.
Suppose that for some guarantee of peace and ease, or some
Other form of happiness, my now taut ideals sag
Letting my life absorb the shocks of joy and rage,

What then? What, indeed, then. I do not know.
To-day my left hand is on my desk and the sun shines on
The long curious fingers that people admire. It is early
To be regretting the things that will be gone,
The fine-drawn skin, the midday sun, the hot ideals that show
Indulgence, lack of integrity or false sympathy rarely.

Yet now, in my twenty-sixth year, the questions are being written down
And the day upon which I must reply draws near.
I have no answers ready; so I am not much surprised
That every sentence strips some nerve of fear,
Or that, walking in streets or sitting in rooms, the sound
Of voices frightens me, their menace being so thinly disguised.

The Gull

Some bitch of a bird yelled dog's abuse
At me this morning when I woke up.
Flat on my back I listened, stunned
By the bad-tempered tirade that never stopped

Once even for breath or to choose a word.
From her tongue's tip a sailor's range
Of invective, blue as the sky, spearing towards me
Slewed and ricochetted against the window pane,

As she made her own of the five-tone scale
With a design of grace-notes no coal-quay shawlie
Could shuffle together on a sunny morning
Or drunk in a pub in an evening's brawling.

This was what I had feared all along;
Trick-o-the-loop Nature, street-angel, house-devil.
Well I guessed the sheen on the far green hills
To be the smooth evil of satin, its moral level.

So, while at the window, a wicked bird frantically
Crumpled the morning tissue of silence, I resolved
To put as much distance between Nature's red claws
And myself as the years could make possible.

For me the Queensberry game, the built-up manner, the artificial,
Will be some vantage-point from which to view the wild,
Afford delaying actions while I make some judgments
Uninfluenced by the terror of a child,

And, in due course, questioned, I'll reply
That the great white bird with the cruel beak was to blame
Who, one sunny quiet morning in May, suddenly frightened me,
Roaring, cursing and spitting against the window-pane.

Elegy for the Commencement of Winter

These apple trees shall be resplendent again
In their pearl-draped vanity, when summer smacks hard
Home in the next year, playing its trump card
After winter's gamble and the spring's slick stratagem.
These bushes, too, the berry and the currant,
Shall swank it through the autumn in their new rig-out,
Swaying their laden shoulders with the seductive, insolent
Assurance of girls in evening dress dining out.

Who would have the heart to speak then of decline?
Not I, nor Elizabeth; although each new summer
For us is not a period of festival, of drumming
Blood flowering and shooting a line
But another warped and rusted leaf to cover
The rich earth of our youth and our horn-mad days
When every note of the clock brought us another lover
Each, and another love-song to phrase.

Now while winter strikes its first-round gong
Bringing all the dryads, crying, from the woods,
If you look carefully, you will see the buds
Curled up snugly in their own warmth.
Already they plan dresses, make their dates, decide
The menus for their roaring parties, engage
The bands that will provide both sweet and jive
When light-fingered spring flicks over another page.

But from me, in this garden, confidence slips like a shawl,
Watching the leaves like damaged gliders toss
And tailspin in the southern warm wind and cut across
The path, between her and the low granite wall,
Knowing the infective evil latent
In their rust, how the disease, contracted, spreads,
The limbs, once cramped, never to be again straightened
Or summer detonate in our heads.

41

By the Dodder in Flood at Herbert Bridge

In this river, flooded by recent rains,
The current sobs heavily like a girl
Watching her day angrily warp and curl
Into scales of white foam like a dragon's mail.
Danger is on tap like oil, insolent, yet all
The olive-green pike, the brilliant-finned perch, behind the wall
Of weeds, where the shallows were, can cower
Grimly, counting their safety out hour by hour.

Looking across the garden towards the river, alone, I think
How for us, flooded by circumstance, no weedy margins
Offer their dubious protection, as we stand, uncertain,
With our hands hanging, by winter's brink,
Yet ours, all spring and summer, was the shrewd concentration
On crops and fuel, preparing for this evil season,
Neither flowers nor birds tempting our attention nor even
Gay girls laughing in the hay-meadows, wheedling.

Silently, in late November, we in this soured land
Wait the Hunger Moon, the days closing in, rain
Gunning the windows, the wind rising, the pain
Of winter already in our numbed hands.
How will we live for the next twelve months
Is the bare question, seeing the results
Of our year's labour, turf-clamps ruined, the tempting
Harvest lost and all our store-houses empty.

1945.

42

Clear View in Summer

Heavy with leaves the garden bushes again
Sun, and the trees admire them, lazily.
Cabbages and carnations, drills and beds of them, droop tiredly
And far away the hills, like dry dogs, crouching, squeal for water.
Love, who is it whispers everything is in order
On this summer afternoon, when nothing moves, not even the flies, strangely,
As we relax by the lawn, here under the pear-tree, watching idly
The leaves declining, the shadows surely lengthen.

But it won't be always summer — not for us; there are bad times coming
When you and I will look with envy on old photographs,
Remembering how we stood, there in the sun, looking like gods,
While the days of our lives, like fruit, swelled and decayed,
And how, by the lake,
Its surface, one August evening, unchipped, walking, we laughed
As love slipped his arms through ours and we gladly followed
The path he showed us through life's valley running.

There'll be much to recall then, when, like wet late summer leaves,
The days under our tread don't rustle, no other summer waiting
Around the turn of a new year with rich clothes to grace us
Whose subtle beauty will have long since languished;
And Nature's flashing greenness will stitch up our hearts with anguish
Each day when August with sunlight riddles the branches, the leaves taking
Voluptuously the south west wind's caresses
Year after dying year.

And yet the declension of each following season, each day's
Defection, splits open our hope only and not our courage, safe and sound
In the deep shelter of our awareness; the bushes and tall trees
Flourish and go down unconsciously in defeat
While full-grown man, whose pride the angels weep,
Watches love itself gutter out some dull evening, nobody around,
Winter moving in, no fuel left, the lights not working, the lease
Unrenewable, summer a seldom-remembered scat-phrase.

Mirage

They had the blind and beautiful eyes of statues
But their bodies had vitality, were eager to be loved,
And all were graceful with a suggestion of swallows;
Since sometimes, then, there seems no end to love
(The night has its own devices and even the day
A trick or two to delude the unwary heart,
Make yearn the fingers, the blood long, the body tentatively shudder)

Why shouldn't the heart, sick with loneliness,
Turn to them naturally as the needle, swinging, turns north
Home to the ice-lidded, lifeless desert covering
The burning magnetic centre of its love,
Wish for warmth in these sodden days, dripping
With fear, hope dirty in the gutters, the horizon of grief
Dragging the road away always, the sinews rotting?

Yet it was heart-breaking, waking to a bright morning
In autumn, watching through the window the leaves take off
In a west wind, turning, to see those eyes, blank, uncomprehending,
And, a gull's harsh voice slithering down your ear-drum,
Know where the truth lay, that you were lonelier than trees
Stripped in winter, no summer consolation of fruition
Yours, not even the spring expectancy.

From New Ross

In this quiet town it is odd to discover
A day buried so deeply in the debris of years
And to dig it out, not damaged at all, discoloured
With dust to be wiped away like tears.
Why here of all places? Was it the fall
Of sunlight on the trees beyond, or the startling call
Of a trumpet unexpectedly down the street, lay
Flush with the memory and pathos of that day?

Say, anyhow, it was: for love like trumpets then
Shattered the walls of our reserve in a sunlit garden
When, over the hedge, you threw the cherries to me and again
Innocence gave us a blessing and a pardon
As little we thought of the fleet, disturbing swallow
Along air-lanes in the garden skidding, stuttering its warning
Of night over the horizon implacably throbbing
With answers both for our laughing and our sobbing.

O Elizabeth, the gold trumpets no more
Curl for you their notes, though the cherry-tree
Each year displays its wares in hope
Your fingers will fondle them caressingly,
And here is my youth, like a bright ribbon, soiled
By death, my days, the dustbin gang, the broken delph, destroyed
By hopes that leave like visitors and leave
A trail of stains that smiling won't conceal.

Yet now, watching the swallows bank over the trees
There where the river bends, suddenly I find time to wonder
What can stop the cough in my life or ease
The choking effects of so many blunders —
Somewhere there should be love aloud like music.
Over the hunching hills, the wires go trailing their furious
Messages, the oiled machinery of nature shunts
Day down for repairs. Silently the night's technicians hunt.

45

Hector

Talking to her, he knew it was the end,
The last time he'd speed her into sleep with kisses:
Achilles had it in for him and was fighting mad.
The roads of his longing she again wandered,
A girl desirable as midsummer's day.

He was a marked man and he knew it,
Being no match for Achilles whom the gods were backing.
Sadly he spoke to her for hours, his heart
Snapping like sticks, she on his shoulder crying.
Yet, sorry only that the meaning eluded him,

He slept well all night, having caressed
Andromache like a flower, though in a dream he saw
A body lying on the sands, huddled and bleeding,
Near the feet a sword in bits and by the head
An upturned, dented helmet.

Icarus

As, even to-day, the airman, feeling the plane sweat
Suddenly, seeing the horizon tilt up gravely, the wings shiver,
Knows that, for once, Daedalus has slipped up badly,
Drunk on the job, perhaps, more likely dreaming, high-flier Icarus,
Head butting down, skidding along the light-shafts
Back, over the tones of the sea-waves and the slip-stream, heard
The gravel-voiced, stuttering trumpets of his heart

Sennet among the crumbling court-yards of his brain the mistake
Of trusting somebody else on an important affair like this;
And, while the flat sea, approaching, buckled into oh! avenues
Of acclamation, he saw the wrong story fan out into history,
Truth, undefined, lost in his own neglect. On the hills,
The summer-shackled hills, the sun spanged all day;
Love and the world were young and there was no ending:

But star-chaser, big-time-going, chancer Icarus
Like a dog on the sea lay and the girls forgot him,
And Daedalus, too busy hammering another job,
Remembered him only in pubs. No bugler at all
Sobbed taps for the young fool then, reported missing,
Presumed drowned, wing-bones and feathers on the tide
Drifting in casually, one by one.

Lackendarragh

I.M. *my friend the poet Bill Clare, d. by drowning 1942*

And it was summer the day — late as usual, the middle
Of August, I think — and I thought how, then, little
    If any should die on a red evening
And hollow-chested Maulin and big-dugged Old Boleys pinned up
       That Sunday right then for me,
          Wishing me more luck
Any day. O it was sweet in the valley gleaming
      With girls to go taunting
And thwarting the evening that night and the next season,
All over the shoulders of Boleys warily peeping.

And lucky was I, knew I it, to cradle my arms round
A sunray at six, in my twenty-first year on the ground,
    The days going down like armies;
But the river was talking fast, you were laughing, I couldn't be bothered
      Thinking how later I'd like to remember
        Odd sunrays like gossip.
Had later been mentioned, I'd only have said, 'What harm is
      It, laughing like this, though September
Be down round the corner?' We were young, we were gay
And rich in the worship of a simple day.

O younger than summer easily, the apple-hung and the berry-studded
Days dropping ripe into our hands, walking the wooded
    Inclines of the valley, we had nothing
To do with death, although around us already, being August, the candles
      Of autumn flared out one by one
        And summer her bangles
Her jewels, her castanets and daring dresses was putting
      Away sorrowfully: all being done
With; we were the last romantics there and then, flaunting
Our hearts asleeve, by the log-bridged river ranting.

Still on the air, though than I older far, the river
Unscripted larks, dayfree now as then, never
        The poor mouth on or a grumble;
But down in the valley this later August grieves,
            I see, the green exotic summer,
                A revelry of leaves
Frittering out ineptly; and I, hearing the black tick in the year, wonder
            When was our tuppeny-coloured
World: the river talks fast but I can't answer,
Knowing now each minute the last one cancels

— Knowing Time, that brings the leaf to book but leaves
A river gabble away a good Sunday any year,
        For winter, the old wound, probes
In the heel of this season. Bleakly the bluff I essay,
            Hoping defeat has its pride
                Whatever it may
Be: for love will be missing in the latter end, an old
            Shoe worn out and cast by,
Left rotting on some forgotten road long before and far away
Over the hills on a perhaps like this religious day.

Time, the Faithless

All evening, while the summer trees were crying
Their sudden realisation of the spring's sad death,
Somewhere a clock was ticking and we heard it here
In the sun-porch, where we sat so long, buying
Thoughts for a penny from each other. Near
Enough it was and loud to make us talk beneath our breath.

And a time for quiet talking it was, to be sure, although
The rain would have drowned the sound of our combined voices.
The spring of our youth that night suddenly dried
And summer filled the veins of our lives like slow
Water into creeks edging. Like the trees you cried.
Autumn and winter, you said, had so many disguises

And how could we be always on the watch to plot
A true perspective for each minute's value? I couldn't reply,
So many of my days toppled into the past, unnoticed.
Silence like sorrow multiplied around you, a lot
Of whose days counted so much. My heart revolted
That time for you should be such a treacherous ally

And though, midnight inclining bells over the city
With a shower of sound like tambourines of Spain
Gay in the teeth of the night air, I thought
Of a man who said the truth was in the pity,
Somehow, under the night's punched curtain, I was lost.
I only knew the pity and the pain.

Poem in the Depths of Summer
for Sheila

Here, now, again, in this garden, I watch the summer
        Burn away, June alight,
The season's torch crackling: and O among the flowers,
        My childhood drumming
        On my memory, nights
And days of red-faced vigour I remember when the hours,
Each one of them a long lane, faced me and, brave
        Child I, I essayed them unafraid.

Gripped in my fist the burning season then each hour's
        Holes and corners lit
Up brightly and slyly I hid myself, chuckling with joy;
        And the roistering flowers
        Through the slits
Of their lives, hopped out and searched for me, a boy
Free as air evading them, shouting and laughing and running
        Round each day's turning.

Lost long since, those days: but, girl, you, who came
        To me with the good
Weather this year, the lamb and the crocus, the birds,
        Have suddenly made
        Them again real. Could
Summer have presented me flowers topping you with your words
Of joy, laughing among the hours, calling to me gaily
        Love is never failing?

Summer flickers down, I know; but, my darling, we
        Have something on tap
To tide us from year to year: a reserve of love
        Deep and free;
        And, though winter, perhaps,
Invest us, here we have sustenance, over and above
Our possible needs — till like trees we blossom
Again, our lives' leaves tossing.

The Invocation

Ten bloody years with this quill lying
Almost idle on my table, I have sourly watched

The narrow summers go, the winters ride over,
Awaiting always, seized in a cold silence,

The genetic word, the arrogant vaticinal line.
And each spring, unmoving by an open window,

The room ringing with emptiness like an unswung bell,
My notebook open, filled with abstract questions,

The bare trees outside expectant, I saw the crocus tell
The indolent fall of the autumn leaves, another year's

Bitter burning and the ice again forming.

Lie with me now, therefore, these wording days,
The ever-questing, tragic-gesturing mind this spring exulting,

Lady I have icily waited for, whom I have known
By these aboding mountains, this lovely glen.

For a Girl on Her Twenty-First Birthday whose Party I Missed

Greetings

Much that you have hitherto learned must be re-examined in the light of a mature mind. And those things, unknown as yet, which will lie in your path must be approached with more circumspection than was your wont when, as an infant, you sported in the sun and made light of the death-agonies of worms. Those who have little virtue to recommend them to civil gentry must be shunned as the abomination or the mouse; for the inhabitants of this island are prone to indolence, yea, sloth, drunkenness and other idle graces.
Apply yourself to your studies, Avril Webb.

Wrap Up My Green Jacket

Wrap up my green jacket in a brown paper parcel
I won't need it now any more,
Now the harp on the green standard low in the dust
Lies covered with mud and with gore,
For deep shall I lie who fell as the flag
Fluttered down on the street and goodbye,
Goodbye to the Oul' Cause we cherished and loved,
We bade with a heart-breaking sigh.

O long by the Liffey I lived out my life,
Minding children and house and fair wife
Till Kathleen Mavourneen called out and one day
Closed down on the lease on my life
And now in the foggy dew, dying, I lie
Regretting the dawn I won't see
As slowly my life's blood stains the brown earth
And slowly my life ebbs from me.

While down from the high cliffs the rivulets teeming
Are calling me sadly away
Oh! never again in this world shall I see
The dawn of a new summer's day.
So, as shines the bright sun and the oul' flag of green
Floats not in the breeze as of yore,
Wrap up my green jacket in a brown paper parcel,
I won't need it now any more.

Note: This song, sung by a dying Irish fighter during the Rising of 1803, to the traditional Irish air *Spailpín a rúin*, is from a radio play of mine with the same title, broadcast three times by the B.B.C. The late Louis Macneice produced the play whilst Betty Chanellor and Cyril Cusack played the parts of Sarah Curran and Robert Emmet respectively. Copyright © Sheila Iremonger who arranged the music.

Sweeney's Short Song Come Candlemas

O lucky the lad whose lass can lilt
A summery song this winter weather
When the ice lies over the loach lake
And the berry dies on the holly bush.

Not dull the day that with delight
The lass can carol her crony home
Though the dunlin keels on its brown back
And the frost nobbles the jenny wren.

Fragment From An Unfinished Poem

Now not any more of summer
This year, its light so golden, all shining, ducking down
　　The reaches of the valley, the leaf-ridden lanes
　　Of my heart, too, with its gold-looking joy
　　　　Stippled and the brown
Earth, like a girl, sung in its warmth, I should think, so
　　Swiftly its din to a murmur
Falls this morning. Rising, I wait for Autumn, as strains
Of Summer's music while up the garden, unhappy again, I go,
　　　　Down the avenues of daylight die.

　　Into the morning siphons
Surely the doom all August, the great-clappered honeysuckle
　　Clanging down the valley, we denied:
　　Slowly, leaf after leaf loosing, calmly,
　　　　Summer so subtly
Its strategic withdrawal devises and Autumn, over these sun-loving broad
　　Acres, melancholy, frightening, silent
Invader, is beamed in gradually; and again, as ever, with a child's
Unease and indecision, I watch, this gloomy Sunday, sloping off,
　　The lovely sun's green armies.

The Old House

Simply to come to it again, having been absent
For many years — marriage, children, the tiring
Duties of provision: things in a dubious world
Themselves worthy enough.

Often he wondered whether the new wing he added
Shortly before he left had a sure foundation,
A good dampcourse; and whether the timber, carefully fitted,
Had been sufficiently seasoned.

Looking at it now from the roadway, it seems to stand
Solidly against the main building, not too brash, ageing
In a dignified reticence as the evening cool sun
Slants over the hill just westward

And along the drive, slowly, as becomes a prodigal
Knowing the family, curious, detached, watching,
Heir now to the whole house and its rich broad acres,
He moves towards possession.

I. M. Edith McFadden

d. aet. 24, 27 June 1950

Littler than I, she has gone on
Brashly into darkness, a slip of a girl.
With her fingers crossed, she scorned
Waiting any longer.

Grey-whiskered Death, our renowned daddy, deployer of all,
Alone knows where she now goes; the gardens fruitlessly echo
To the name of her name, the wind in the trees
Ceaselessly vowelling it . . .

Chider of angels, your humble servant,
Kneeling, discreetly distant, meticulously asking,
This bleak midsummer day, for this lost girl,
That famous mercy, the sward outside
In its order receptively disturbed, the broken
Vase of her laughter scattered across it carelessly.

Footnote To Marxism

for Christine, 1952

> He liked to play games with his children . . . .
> Edmund Wilson: *To the Finland Station.*

The bucking children on the sitting room floor,
The scattered toys, the dog-eared children's books,
The furniture shoved in any convenient nook,
The table on its end against the door
Draped in a grey camping blanket as a kind
Of hide-out, staff headquarters or simple eating-joint
(The purpose varying with demands of action, the points
For decision or the stolid needs of time)

— This Marx-like setting shows us a roughly honest world
Where shades of meaning, subtle and clever phrasing
Such as concern the scholar who owns the table
Are uncalled for. The logical accurate words
That spang around the room convey the exact sense
They are meant to, in a strictly present tense.

Jane Browne

Jane Browne had red hair that dazzled
The boys in Sandymount when she was even eight.
Going from school, all would be eager
Politely to see her to the garden gate

And, anxious to please, until she reached the door
Where she turned on the step and waved goodbye,
They waited; as ten years later they waited
Patiently on her with love-struck sighs.

Each was delighted with her merest favour,
Missing the mockery in her modest eyes
As she bent for a light or her mischievous laughter
Tinkled in the moony sky.

God love you, Miss Jane Browne. I had forgotten
Your pale cheeks, your smile, your red hair,
Our walks by Marlay, our melancholy love-glances,
Our kiss on the darkened stair . . . .

And I would have had it like that; for when someone today
Said you died during a bitter war in pain,
Twenty years crashed down around me like gravel
And suddenly the garden daffodils were bursting around you again

As over your gate in married middle age
Memory leaned in grief. The reflecting mind
Marked off not empty minutes but those years
Of silence by your absence now defined.

The Eve Of Destruction

for Suds and Gibbles

One daffodil
So brilliantly yellow,
Its head hanging over
On a piece of waste ground
In this cruel arctic April.

Two cosmonauts
In space now.
Let's pretend, darlings,
We don't know
What they're doing.

Marginalia these words, maybe,
Such as the old wise
Monks left us.

For the record, then,
If it survives,
I'm sorry our grandchildren
Won't be able even to

See

Such a yellow
Daffodil.

Stockholm 1966.

Before the End

Just keep on saying
No.

Tape it and attach
The tape to the telephone
To save your breath:
Slag down to the boozer
For what may be positively, definitely,
(You know how these things are)
Your Final Appearance
And your last drink.

Every time you're asked
To fill up a form
Scribble the word down twice

— In the margin always.

Not all that good, daughter,
In the latter end for you

— Speaking personally
I mean
You.

I, of course,
Am mooching off
Down to World's End
For a drink.
They're after me, too.

The writing is on the wall
In blood this time

Some of it yours, some mine,

Daughter.

Stockholm
Valborgsnatt 1966.

Note: World's End is an area in South-West London.

Due to a Technical Fault

Three days gone now
And no letters.

They've stopped delivery because
It doesn't matter any more

To them or to
Us.

Communication is through.

I don't know what's happening
Do you?

Over there in Mount Pleasant
They're counting sacks of mail

Not, of course
For you
Or me.

What a life of idle grace
They're having.

Tomorrow
Will be the fourth day.

Will anything happen

Tonight?

Stockholm

Note: Mount Pleasant is the
London postal sorting office.

On Some Boiler

at the Delhi Station

The vulture on the tree in the garden,
A close eye on the six labrador pups;

The mynah bird, strutting, preening and squealing,
My younger daughters strutting, preening and squealing;

John Montague, a bullying friend in Paris, worried,
Me in New Delhi, worried;

Kevin Nowlan, a professional historian,
Addressing a demo from a balcony

In a worthy cause;
Roger McHugh in the lotus position this minute

Staring at an oval-faced geisha girl, and explaining
The philosophical nature of Noh;

Martin Sheridan, reverentially excoriating
In the name of the Lord, *la condition humaine;*

Harry Boylan, saturnine in a sailing boat,
Some obscure gaelic saying on his lips as the mast breaks;

Conor Cruise O'Brien, a Voltaire cultivating his garden
At Whitewater where we were all so happy

Sometime; across the bay, lovely Sandymount
Where we were all so happy sometime;

The thunder breaks now in Delhi: Montague arrives
Again, as ever, a Northern chip on his shoulder

And breaking old moulds.

These friends:
Intelligible realities — the food for contemplation.

The Master Plan

In the beginning
You lie on your back,
Eyes closed,
Arms tentatively moving,
An occasional cry.

Later, tossing and turning
For many years,
You wonder at the apparently
Haphazard movements of life,
Of nature, of joys,
Of griefs, humiliations,
Of memories too many to count.

In the end
You lie on your back,
Eyes closed,
Arms over chest stilled,
No cry at all.

Sandymount Now

for Frank Biggar

No one should go
Back to the old places.
Too many one knew
Are dead,
Old slow remembered customs
Gone with them.

And the streets, besides,
Seem narrower
In any event.
The Green tidied up
By the Municipal Council,
The rough fields covered
By semi-detacheds
With tiny gardens,
The teeming tumultuous sea
Pushed further back
By a new wall;
All disturbing elements
Pretty nearly
Accounted for

— Including, alas,
Regret,
Which, at any time,
Is irrelevant.

Horan's Field

In torn ganseys, patched worsted pants, we played
Seven-a-side rugby in winter there.
We had no goal-posts — a few ganseys
Pulled off as we warmed up
Did to make goal at each end of the pitch.
Touch was if the ball hit
The back walls of the houses
Fifty yards off on one side. On the other side,
Touch was where the ball was canted
Into the plots where needy people,
Like our parents, were allocated
Patches of ground to grow vegetables in
— Cheaper than shop-buying.

The field was owned by Mr. Horan, the butcher
— Blue pinafore, blue and white striped apron,
A cleaver, meat-saw or meat-knife
Perpetually in his hand as he hacked
Hunks of steak from cow, sheep, calf
Carcases hanging behind him, his hands
Red with liver-blood (a favourite
Delicacy in Sandymount —
Liver, I mean, not blood).
A decent man, Mr. Horan, who died,
As we all do, too soon.

Monkstown Third Fifteen
Played there every Saturday.
We were proud to call ourselves
Monkstown Fourths — without authority
Of any kind save the normal human
Desire for aggrandisement.
I played fly-half and Tommy
Scrum-half. Ball under my arm,
Rushing for the goal-line,

Like the Gaels going forth to battle,
I always fell. Being tackled invariably
By Louis was like being run
Down by a medium-sized tank.
I never scored, not once.

On the houses' side of the field
Was waste ground — moundy, scutch-grassed,
Overlaid here and there with
Cast out sheets of corrugated tin,
Rusty, holed and easy to cut yourself on.
Skeletons of what once had been
Prams holding the family pride,
Bits of old car doors,
— We used these to make dug-outs
For our serious gang-warfare with other
Boys from the village even more
Tattered and torn than we were.

At one end of this waste ground
Was a wall which we frequently climbed
And sat astride to admire
A formal garden such as we knew
We would never have — roses, tulips, sweetpea,
Daffodils, gladioli, chrysanthemums
(Whatever was in season),
Apple trees, goosegob, raspberry, strawberry bushes
— All the delights of envious childhood.
We sat there until the owner came
And ordered us down. It was a constant
Amazement to us such a garden's owner
Should dispense
Porter in the dirtiest pub in the village.

There was another house, barrack-like,
With nothing in the garden
Save the well-kept lawn
And a few trees.
Over the wall we gazed

In horrified fascination at the house,
Garden and out-houses. It was
An experimental Veterinary Station.
We knew the owner had hundreds
Of white rabbits locked up in cages
In the outhouses for some diabolical
Purposes.
We could hear the rabbits squealing.
We shared their locked-up agony,
We shared it and vowed
Retributive vengeance sometime.
In the meantime, we stole the vet's apples.

It was not, however, all pains, aches
And agony. I had a twelve-year-old's love
For tubby, tousle-headed, red-haired Marise
(Tommy preferred sloe-eyed, raven-haired Betty).
Lying there in the field at the end
Nearest the strand — only a one-foot,
Broken-down wall behind us —
We relaxed holding innocent hands.
Flat on our backs, she pretty in her
Blue tailored gym-slip, me caked in mud
From the hour-long game, we gazed
Straight up at the clear blue sky
(I cannot recall rain, fog or cloudy skies
In those astonishing days).
In time, to avoid parental trouble,
We went home to do our homework.
At six o'clock the day was over.

Where are Marise and Betty now?
Sean, Pudgy, Builder, Ledser,
Kitty, Celia, Margaret, Finn,
Fisher, Luger, Mooner, Eve?
The girls, I suppose, are married,
The boys too, and stuck half-way
Through a desk like myself.

70

We were famous people in our day
And to all and to the boy
I feel now holding this pen,
I send my reminiscent love.
Marise, Marise, the world is at us all.
It falls upon us like a Himálayan peak
And we are trapped, no hope at all,
The rope broken, the crampons gone.
Above, above, a persuasive sky
But now no way back for homework.
Marise, Marise, the best is yet to be,
We're told — that solemn grown-ups' fantasy.

We boxed on the waste ground too,
An elimination contest every quarter.
I wasn't much good but once,
By staying out of punishment's way,
Running backwards to a hump in the ground
Where I knew I could fall accidentally, convincingly,
I managed to collect enough points,
In avoiding Pudgy's flailing fists,
To get me to the quarter final.
The two best fighters were Pudgy
And Butcher Boy (he wore butcher-blue suits).
Butcher Boy ran away from home at fourteen
Because his mother beat him regularly
Every day for his own good; and he couldn't hit back.
He joined the British Army,
Is believed killed in the last war.

Horan's field is gone now, a mass
Of handkerchief-lawned semi-detacheds
Covers it
This thirty-five years.
The one-foot broken wall,
The sandy mounds that faced the sea's dark
Winter anger, gone. The new sea-wall

71

Efficiently controls the tides until
They
Get around to abolishing the strand
Altogether, entirely, shortly.

Slowly, night comes to Sandymount,
Soon like Horan's field to be abolished also
When the land is sold, the old
Victorian and Edwardian modest
Family houses demolished,
Making way for tall stately
Office blocks,
Their square skulls
Gazing out confidently to the retreated sea,

The village, like childhood, only remembered
By old faded photographs.

Marise . . . .

New Delhi, 1969.

VERSIONS
mainly from Irish

Clonmel Prison

O a year from tomorrow I left my own people,
I went down to Ardpatrick, the ribbons in my hat.
Some Whiteboys were there then, they were fighting the English
And now I'm sad and lonely in Clonmel's foul prison.

My bridle and saddle are gone from me this long time,
My hurley well hidden behind my own door,
My slither's being played with by the boys of the valley
The one I could hit a goal with as good as another.

O Kerrymen, please pray for me, soft and lovely were your voices,
Little I thought ever that I never would return to you
And to think our three heads will be spiked and on show here
In the snows of the winter's night and any other weather that comes to us.

To Iveragh if you ever go, take the news to my people
That I'm lost to this world now and will be dead beyond Friday.
Make sure there's a good wake for me, a good coffin to carry me in:
That's the end of O'Donnell and forever say a prayer for him.

from the Irish
Trans. V.I.

The Blaskets

The great sea under the sun will lie like a mirror,
Not a boat sailing, not a living sign from a sinner,
The golden eagle aloft in the distance, the last
Vestige of life by the ruined abandoned Blaskets.

The sun will be gone, the shadow of night spreading
As the moon, rising, through a cloud coldly stretches
Its ghostly fingers over the silent earth
Where, wracked, the shells of the houses stand deserted

— Silent save for the birds all homeward flying
Glad to be back, their heads on their breasts lying,
And the wind soughing, softly a half-door swinging
By cold wet hearths, their fires forever extinguished.

BRENDAN BEHAN
Trans. V.I.

Thanks be to Joyce

Here in the rue St. André des Arts
In an Arab tavern, pissed,
For a studious Frenchman I construe you,
For ex-G.I.'s and a Russian, pissed.
All of those things you penned I praise
As, in France, I drink Pernod in return.
Proud of you as a writer we are
And grateful for the Calvados we owe to you.

If you were me
And I were you
Leaving Les Halles
Holding all this cognac
On a full belly bawling
You'd write a verse or two in my praise.

BRENDAN BEHAN
Trans. V.I.

76

Oscar

After all the strife
That, alive, he caused,
Ravaged with fear,
In the half-light stretched,
The gay spark's body
Lies dumb in the dark,
Silent, the funereal
Candles guttering,
The graceful body,
The firm gaze, spent
In a cold bare room
With a concierge spiteful
From too much attendance
On a foreign tippler
Who left without paying
The ten per cent service.
Exiled from the Flore
To a saintly desert
The young prince of sin
A withered churl
The gold jewel of lust
Left far behind him.
No pernod to brace him
Only holy water
— The young king of Beauty,
A ravished narcissus
As the star of the pure Virgin
Glows on the water.

Envoi

Delightful the path of sin
But a holy death's a habit.
Good man yourself there, Oscar:
Every way you had it.

BRENDAN BEHAN
Trans. V.I.

King Sweeney's Valediction

Suibhne or Sweeney, King of Dal Araidhe in Ireland,
treacherously kills one of St. Ronan's acolytes during
the battle of Moira in A.D. 637. As a result of St.
Ronan's curse, Sweeney goes out of his mind and
spends the rest of his life wandering throughout Ireland
stark naked and living in the trees. In his turn, he is
treacherously injured and, as he lies dying in the arms
of St. Moling, he makes this lay:

Sweeter far to me once
Than the tranquil conversing of my kindred,
The churkling of the turtle-dove
Swooping over the pool.

Sweeter far to me once
Than the sound of the prayer-bell beside me,
The melody of the blackbird on the cliff,
The stag belling in the tempest.

Sweeter far to me once
Than the voice of a beautiful woman beside me,
The cry of the gorse on the mountain
Heard after rising.

Sweeter far to me once
The howl of the wolf-pack
Than the voice of the cleric within
Lowing and bleating.

Though you relished your pot-houses
And your sumptuous ale-feasts,
I preferred a draught of clear water
Drunk from the palm out of a well.

Though sweet to you in your church there
The calm discoursing of your students,
Sweeter to me the pleasant paean
Sung by the hounds of Glen Bolcain.

78

Though you relished the salt meat and the fresh
Eaten in your assembly houses,
I preferred a fistful of fresh cress
Eaten somewhere carelessly.

The cruel herd's spear has wounded me
Travelling clean through my body.
A Pity, O Christ who gives every judgment,
That I was not killed at Moira.

Though good every bed in truth
I made around Ireland,
I'd prefer a bed over the lake
In the open Mourne mountains.

Though good every bed in truth
I made around Ireland
I'd prefer the bed in the wood
That I made in Glen Bolcain.

I give thanks after that
For partaking, O Christ, of your body,
Truly repenting on earth
For every evil deed I have done.

from the Irish
Trans. V.I.

79

Carmen XI

Furi et Aureli, comites Catulli . . .

Furius and Aurelius, buddies of Catullus,
Whether he is exploring the outer Indies
Where, constantly echoing, the appropriate seas
    Smash on the shore,

Or whether he is in the Near East among the shifty Arabs
Or in Central Asia among the well-heeled Parthians
Or where the seven-fingered Nile
    Massages the desert,

Or even if he goes over the frozen Alps
Viewing the marvellous work of the great Caesar
— Right along the Rhine and even among the really
    Unspeakable British,

My true friends, ready to face such specific dangers
Shoulder to shoulder with me, and even unknown other perils,
Are you ready now to take over to my girl-friend
    A short and bitter note:

May she live and rot with her lechers
And may she give three hundred of them some night
The same routine, leaving them all
    Burnt up the same way.

She need not, as long ago, worry about my love
Which she has killed herself — just as the flower
At the edge of the field by the plough
    Is savaged and abandoned.

CATULLUS
Trans. V.I.